The Princedom of Pea

A Readers' Theater Script and Guide

Readers' Theater
How to Put on a Production

By Nancy K. Wallace • Illustrated by Nina Mata

magic wagon

visit us at www.abdopublishing.com

To my daughters, Mollie and Elizabeth, who have spent endless hours helping with library plays! —NKW

Published by Magic Wagon, a division of the ABDO Group, PO Box 398166, Minneapolis, Minnesota 55439. Copyright © 2014 by Abdo Consulting Group, Inc. International copyrights reserved in all countries. All rights reserved. No part of this book may be reproduced in any form without written permission from the publisher.

Looking Glass Library™ is a trademark and logo of Magic Wagon.

Printed in the United States of America, North Mankato, Minnesota.
042013
092013
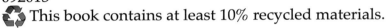 This book contains at least 10% recycled materials.

Written by Nancy K. Wallace
Illustrations by Nina Mata
Edited by Stephanie Hedlund and Rochelle Baltzer
Cover and interior design by Renée LaViolette

Library of Congress Cataloging-in-Publication Data
Wallace, Nancy K.
  The princedom of pea : a readers' theater script and guide / by Nancy K. Wallace ; Illustrated by Nina Mata.
      p. cm. -- (Readers' theater: how to put on a production)
  ISBN 978-1-61641-988-2
1. Fairy tales--Adaptations--Juvenile drama. 2. Theater--Production and direction--Juvenile literature. 3. Readers' theater--Juvenile literature. I. Mata, Nina, 1981- II. Andersen, H. C. (Hans Christian), 1805-1875. Prindsessen paa ærten. III. Title.
  PS3623.A4436P87 2013
  812'.6--dc23
                    2013006052

Table of Contents

School Plays

Do you like to act, create props, make weird sound effects, or paint scenery? You should put on a production. Plays are lots of fun. And a play is a great way for kids to work together as a team.

Readers' theater can be done very simply. You just read your lines. You don't have to memorize them! Adapted readers' theater looks more like a regular play. The performers wear makeup and costumes. The stage has scenery and props. The cast moves around to show the action. But, performers can still read their scripts.

Does your class need to raise money for a trip? Does your library need money to buy new books? Plays can also be fund-raisers. You can sell tickets to your production and raise money for a good cause!

You will need a space large enough to put on your production. An auditorium with a stage is ideal. A classroom will work, too. Now, choose a date and get permission to use the space.

Finally, make flyers or posters to advertise your play. Place them around your school and community. Tell your friends and family. Everyone enjoys watching kids perform!

Cast & Crew

There are many people needed to put on a production. First, decide who will play each part. All of the performers should practice their lines. Reading your lines aloud will help you learn them.

The Princedom of Pea needs the following cast:

Narrator - The storyteller

Queen Patricia - A queen with a bossy attitude

Prince Peter - The queen's son

Princess Penelope Rose - A beautiful princess

Herald - A funny character that carries a banner

Pack of Princesses - At least seven girls that do not speak

Next, a crew is needed. The show can't go on without these important people! Some jobs can be combined for a small show. Every show needs a director. This person organizes everything and everyone in the show.

The director will work with the production crew. This includes the costume designers, who borrow or make all the costumes. Stage managers make sure things run smoothly.

Your production can also have a stage crew. This includes lighting designers to run spotlights and other lighting. Set designers plan and make scenery. Prop managers find or make props for the show. The special effects crew takes care of sound and other unusual effects.

Sets & Props

At a readers' theater production, the performers sit on stools at the front of the room. But, an adapted readers' theater production or full play will require some sets and props.

Sets include a background for each scene of the play. Props are things you'll need during the play. You'll also need tickets that list important information. Be sure to include the title of the play and where it will take place. List the date and time of your performance. Print the price of the ticket if you are charging a fee to attend.

Your production can also have a playbill. It is a printed program. The front of a playbill has the title, date, and time of the play. Playbills list all of the cast and production team members inside.

The Princedom of Pea could have the following set and props:

Scene Sets - A castle made from cardboard painted to look like a stone wall, a flower garden from more painted cardboard, and a fireplace created by cutting into a cardboard box and placing three real logs and orange LED lights inside it. Find a small table and three chairs to use for the dining room.

Props - A felt banner with the letter *P* on it for the herald to carry, a giant letter *P* made out of cardboard, three bowls full of peas, and three spoons.

Makeup & Costumes

The stage and props aren't the only things people will be looking at in your play! The makeup artist has a big job. Stage makeup needs to be brighter and heavier than regular makeup. Buy basic colors of mascara, foundation, blush, and lipstick. Apply with a new cotton ball or swab for each cast member. Even boys wear stage makeup!

Costume designers set the scene just as much as set designers. They borrow costumes or adapt old clothing for each character. For example, make a cloak out of a length of fabric gathered at the neck. Ask adults if you need help finding or sewing costumes.

The Princedom of Pea performers will need these costumes:

Narrator - A shirt and pants with a cloak

Queen Patricia - A long dress and a crown

Prince Peter - A shirt with a fancy vest and a crown

Princess Penelope Rose - A long dress and a cloak

Herald - A uniform with a shirt and pants of the same color, include
    a funny hat with a feather on it

Pack of Princesses - A party dress and a crown for each princess

Stage Directions

When your sets, props, and costumes are ready, it is important to rehearse. Choose a time that everyone can attend. Try to have at least five or six rehearsals before your show.

You should practice together as a team even if you will be reading your scripts for readers' theater. A play should sound like a conversation. Try to avoid pauses when no one is speaking. You can do this by adding sound effects. The sound designer for *The Princedom of Pea* could play music for the party. Let it fade away as the princesses leave the stage. Also, a horn should blow each time the herald walks across the stage.

Some theater terms may seem strange. The *wings* are the sides of the stage that the audience can't see. The *house* is where the audience sits. The *curtains* refers to the main curtain at the front of the stage.

When reading your script, the stage directions are in parentheses. They are given from the performer's point of view, not the audience's. You will be facing the audience when you are performing. Left will be on your left and right will be on your right. When rehearsing, perform the stage directions and the lines to get used to moving around the stage.

right wing

left wing

upstage right

right center

downstage right

upstage center

center stage

downstage center

upstage left

left center

downstage left

Script: *The Princedom of Pea*

(Opening of Curtain: A giant letter "P" stands on or above the stage in plain sight. The stage is set with a dining room table, chairs, and fireplace. Queen Patricia and Prince Peter at center stage near table, and Herald at downstage left. Narrator stationed on stool at downstage left through entire production.)

Narrator: Once upon a time, there was a beautiful island. Its fields were green and fertile. It was cool and rainy all year long, a climate that was just perfect for growing peas! In fact, peas were the national vegetable, the main export, and the Princedom of Pea's only claim to fame.

Herald: *(The herald stands at downstage left with his banner and walks across the stage in front of the other actors as he delivers his line and stops at downstage right.)* Peas for breakfast! Peas for lunch! Peas for dinner! Munch! Munch! Munch! Long live the Princedom of Pea!

Narrator: Now, the Princedom of Pea was ruled by Queen Patricia. She had one son named Peter. When Prince Peter turned 18 years old, his mother thought it was time for him to marry.

Herald: *(The herald stands downstage right and walks across the stage in front of the other actors as he delivers his line and stops at downstage left. He should repeat walking back and forth each time this line is delivered for the rest of the play.)* Peas for breakfast! Peas for lunch! Peas for dinner! Munch! Munch! Munch! Long live the Princedom of Pea!

Queen: We are having a big party. I have sent out invitations to all the eligible princesses in the land. After I have met each of them, I will choose your future wife.

Prince: Oh dear. How many princesses are there?

Queen: Dozens.

Prince: Can't I choose my own wife?

Queen: Don't be silly, darling. Mothers always know best! I will look until I find a princess who is just perfect to rule the Princedom of Pea by your side.

Herald: Peas for breakfast! Peas for lunch! Peas for dinner! Munch! Munch! Munch! Long live the Princedom of Pea!

Narrator: *(Music plays softly. A group of princesses enter from left wing at upstage left.)* And so dozens of princesses came to the palace for the party. But, the queen didn't think any of them were perfect for Prince Peter.

Queen: *(Pointing)* Too tall, too short, too thin, too meek, too mouthy! And that girl's name doesn't even begin with *P*. Send them all home! *(Princesses exit upstage right into right wing.)*

Prince: I thought some of them were very nice.

Queen: *(Waving her hand)* You are only a boy—what would you know? The future of the Princedom of Pea is at stake!

Herald: Peas for breakfast! Peas for lunch! Peas for dinner! Munch! Munch! Munch! Long live the Princedom of Pea!

Queen: Send for a bowl of peas, please! I need a snack! *(Exit all.)*

Narrator: *(Waving toward stage right at a princess who is knocking on air)* That night, there had been a terrible storm. One of the princesses had trouble on the road. She missed the party. She came to the palace long after all the servants had gone to bed. The prince heard her knocking and opened the door himself.

Princess: I was invited to the palace for the party, but the wheel on my coach broke. Then there was this terrible storm. Please, could you let me come in?

Prince: Of course. You must be freezing. Stand over here by the fire and get warm.

Princess: You are very kind.

Narrator: Even in her wet traveling cloak, the prince thought the princess was very pretty. He hoped that maybe this might be the girl that would please his mother. He introduced himself.

Prince: Hello, I'm Prince Peter.

Princess: *(Bowing)* Oh, I'm so glad to meet you! My name is Princess Rose!

Narrator: The prince's heart sank. His mother had only invited princesses to the party whose names began with "P." She would never think that a princess named Rose was suitable to rule the Princedom of Pea.

Herald: Peas for breakfast! Peas for lunch! Peas for dinner! Munch! Munch! Munch! Long live the Princedom of Pea!

Prince: I'll call the servants and have a room prepared for you. In the morning, I will introduce you to my mother.

Narrator: And so Princess Rose spent the night at the palace. Prince Peter spent the night dreaming about her sweet smile and her beautiful face. In the morning, they all gathered in the dining room for breakfast.

Prince: Mother, this is Princess Rose. She arrived late last night. Her coach broke down on the road and she missed the party.

Queen: Princess Rose? Princess Rose? I can't imagine why I invited you to the party. Your name doesn't even begin with "P!"

Princess: Actually it does, Your Majesty. My name is Penelope Rose, but my father always calls me Rose.

Queen: Oh, well that is quite a different matter, then. Come and sit beside me, my dear. Let's get to know each other better.

Narrator: And so they sat down to a breakfast of creamed peas. The queen liked Penelope Rose very much and so did the prince. After a lunch of fresh pea salad, Prince Peter took the princess for a walk. They went to see the gardens of snow peas and green peas and sweet peas.

Princess: *(Exit Queen Patricia, herald, prince, and princess walking downstage right away from table)* Don't you grow anything but peas?

Prince: Of course not! After all, this is the Princedom of Pea.

Herald: Peas for breakfast! Peas for lunch! Peas for dinner! Munch! Munch! Munch! Long live the Princedom of Pea!

Princess: So you don't ever eat anything except peas?

Prince: What else would we eat?

Princess: Well, in my kingdom we eat potatoes, beans, corn, lettuce, and squash. There are all kinds of other vegetables and fruits, too!

Prince: There are? I wonder if my mother knows this. I have never eaten anything but peas and I don't think she has either.

Narrator: That night at dinner, the cook served split pea soup. And the prince told his mother about the other kinds of vegetables.

Queen: I've never heard of such a thing! Everyone eats peas!

Princess: I would be glad to have my father send you some samples of some of our other vegetables. I think you would like the fruits as well, Your Majesty.

Queen: But this is the Princedom of Pea, my dear.

Herald: Peas for breakfast! Peas for lunch! Peas for dinner! Munch! Munch! Munch! Long live the Princedom of Pea!

Queen: Nothing will grow here but peas! It's cool and rainy and perfect for peas!

Princess: I think that potatoes and cabbage would grow here, Your Majesty. And also roses.

Prince: What are roses?

Princess: They are beautiful flowers, Your Majesty. They are even more beautiful than the blossoms on your sweet peas.

Queen: What nonsense is this? There is nothing more beautiful than a sweet pea in bloom!

Narrator: The rest of the meal did not go well. The queen sat in stony silence even though Penelope and Peter continued to talk together. That night, after the princess had gone out onto the balcony for a look at the moon, the queen spoke to Prince Peter alone. *(Princess exit upstage right.)*

Queen: It is time to
send this girl home.
I'm not even certain
she is a real princess.

Prince: Well, of course
she is a princess!
You invited her. She
simply arrived too
late for the party.

Queen: That is what
she told you. You are
so young, my darling. Don't be fooled by a pretty face. No one
can rule the Princedom of Pea along with you but a true princess.

Herald: Peas for breakfast! Peas for lunch!

Queen: Oh, knock it off and go to bed!

Herald: (*Bowing*) Yes, Your Majesty!

Prince: I like Penelope Rose a lot. I would like to choose her as my wife.

Queen: If there is any choosing, I will do it! I have the perfect way to tell if Penelope Rose is truly a princess. Princesses are very sensitive creatures. Tonight you will hide a pea under her mattress. Only a true princess would feel a pea through a mattress. If she sleeps badly tonight, then we will know she is a princess and you can marry her.

Prince: Oh thank you, Mother!

Queen: She hasn't passed the test yet. I'll bet your Penelope will sleep like a baby and tomorrow morning she'll be packing to go home!

Narrator: Prince Peter was beginning to realize he could never marry Penelope unless he took matters into his own hands.

Prince: (*Grabbing the giant letter P in front of the stage*) My mother asked for a *P* and that's what I will put under Penelope's mattress. Even a peasant would have difficulty sleeping on this!

Narrator: The next morning, everyone gathered in the dining room for creamed peas on toast. Penelope arrived yawning. She had dark circles under her eyes and she looked very tired. The prince began to smile.

29

Prince: Why, Penelope, what is the matter?

Princess: Oh, Your Majesty, I don't like to complain. But last night my mattress felt so lumpy and bumpy that I couldn't sleep a wink. I am exhausted!

Queen: I don't believe it! Your mattress was lumpy?

Princess: Yes, Your Majesty. It was fine the night before. I can't imagine what happened to it.

Queen: It just shows that you are a true princess, my dear. My son placed a tiny pea under your mattress last night. You are so sensitive that it felt like a rock to you!

Princess: It did feel like a rock—a very large one, indeed. Are you sure it was just a pea?

Prince: *(Nodding and smiling)* Quite certain. I put it there myself!

Queen: I had to make certain you were a real princess before I asked you to join our family here in the Princedom of Pea.

Princess: I'm not sure I understand, Your Majesty.

Prince: Perhaps I can explain. Princess Penelope Rose, will you marry me?

Princess: Why yes, Prince Peter, I will!

Narrator: And so they were married. Gradually Princess Rose brought changes to the Princedom of Pea. She taught her subjects to grow potatoes, beans, and other vegetables and fruits. Prince Peter started a rose garden to remind his subjects of the beautiful princess he had married. And he kept the letter *P* on the mantel to remind him to always think for himself.

The End

Adapting Readers' Theater Scripts

Readers' theater can be done very simply. You just read your lines. You don't have to memorize them! Performers sit on chairs or stools. They read their parts without moving around.

Adapted Readers' Theater
This looks more like a regular play. The performers wear makeup and costumes. The stage has scenery and props. The cast moves around to show the action. Performers can still read their scripts.

Hold a Puppet Show
Some schools and libraries have puppet collections. Students make the puppets be the actors. Performers can read their scripts.

Teacher's Guides

Readers' Theater Teacher's Guides are available online! Each guide includes reading levels for each character and additional production tips for each play. Visit Teacher's Guides at **www.abdopublishing.com** to get yours today!